Discover Your Purpose

A Simple Guide to Setting and Reaching Your Goals

By: Angelique McTyre

www.A-Meaningful-Life-Today.com
ISBN 978-0-6151-8315-2

This book is dedicated to my life, my love, my daughter…

Desiree Hope Simpson

This book is dedicated to my life, my love, my daughter…

Desiree Hope Simpson

Preface

Life can be so difficult at times. There are so many choices we can make, and so many roads we can follow. It's no wonder why many of us find it hard to decide what to do with our lives. How can we be sure we're on the right path? How do we know we're making the right decisions? How can we be certain we're doing what's best for our lives?

These are just a few of the questions we have about life that seem to go unanswered. It makes us frustrated. Confused. Scared. Angry. Why can't the answers come more easily? Sometimes, I wonder if maybe we're just failing to ask the right question. Maybe our certainty in life comes not from knowing which path to take, but from knowing our destination – our end result. Maybe all we need to do is stop and ask ourselves: "What am I looking for?"

We all want to be happy. We all want to make the most of our lives. To do this, we have to engage ourselves in those specific actions that will lead us toward a *desired* result. We have to know where we're going – and plan our actions accordingly. When we do, we increase not only our sense of certainty, but also our chances at finding personal success, lifelong fulfillment, and ultimately, our true happiness.

Goal-setting is a method of planning. It helps you plan your actions *according* to your desired result. It helps you identify which actions will lead you where you want to go. In *Discover Your Purpose*, I will introduce to you a goal-setting process that is simple and effective – but also unique. It is based on my personal belief that we are all born with certain, instinctive desires to do the following:

- To know and understand ourselves.
- To better ourselves.
- To express ourselves in our own unique way.
- To achieve – by doing what we love and enjoy.
- To love, care for, and help each other.

These desires –our *principle desires* – form the context we must use to define our desired result. When we fail to fulfill these desires, we experience a void, an emptiness in our lives (perhaps you feel it now). This void can not be filled with money, fame, power, or material possessions. It can only be filled with the results that come from a conscious choice to act in accordance with these desires. In *Discover Your Purpose*, my aim is to help you align your goals with these principle desires and develop a stronger commitment toward reaching your goals. With every exercise you complete, you'll be creating a personal plan that will lead you toward your desired result, and the happiness you've been looking for.

PLEASE NOTE: *Discover Your Purpose* is NOT a book of answers. It is a book of questions – designed to help you define the path for your life. Your answers to these questions – provided they are honest and sincere – will point you in a direction that is just right for YOU!

So, release your fears and look forward to a future by *your* design. Today is the day you make a conscious choice to make the most of your life. It is time to take that first step. The only requirement is to trust in, and be true to YOU. Now, let the journey begin…

Table of Contents

Introduction

Happiness – No Fears, No Regrets, and a Sense of Purpose.

Purpose is the *foundation* of true happiness. It brings meaning to life and makes life worth living. Purpose provides a *reason* for your existence, and a *reason* to face each day with courage, confidence, and joy. A life with a well-defined purpose will award you a sense of happiness that can never be known from just living life day-to-day. To find *true* happiness you must not be a slave to mindless routine and a passionless existence. You must define your purpose to discover *how* to make the most of your life.

Defining Your Purpose

If you believe there is a reason for everything, you should believe there is a reason for you. When searching for your purpose in life, you are ultimately asking the question, "Why am I here?" This is a common question, but the answer is not the same for all of us. Each of us is responsible for defining our own purpose in life – how we will use our unique, personal gifts to serve ourselves and others, in our own unique way. The way in which you serve is a personal choice, limited only by your imagination and creativity. You can serve in any facet of life, and in various ways – it's all in how you choose to do it. Your service *is* your purpose. And it is a matter of choice. In this regard, the answer to "Why am I here?" is strictly up to you.

How do you define your purpose? First, consider our *principle desires*. **To know and understand yourself. To better yourself. To express yourself in your own unique way. To achieve by doing what you love and enjoy. To love, care for, and help each other.** Each of these factors should contribute to your life's purpose. They must become the focal point for how you live each day of your life. However, it's up to you to decide *how* you will apply them in your life.

Secondly, recognize what makes you who you are – your unique combination of talents, strengths, passions, concerns, and life experiences. This is part of the Master Plan, if you will. You were created this particular way for a reason. This combination gives you something you can offer the world that no one else can in quite the same way. What you choose to do with this gift is what makes your life meaningful and gives it purpose. You *define* your purpose **by recognizing your unique abilities, acknowledging your *principle desires*, and choosing these gifts will be used in your life**.

Defining Purpose with Principle

Purpose requires a context of some kind – a guiding principle that tells you, in no uncertain terms: **"This is what I stand for and believe in. This is what I value and live for. This is why I do what I do."** Without this context in life, you will *almost certainly* find yourself lost. Before you know it, you'll be caught up in doing for the sake of doing. Soon, you'll discover that what you've *been* doing doesn't matter as much as it did before. Then, you'll regret the time you've lost, doing what really had no significance to you. To define a purpose that is meaningful, you must embrace and understand one critical idea: Your life is not all about YOU.

Your guiding principle should reflect an understanding that we are here on earth to live our lives not only for ourselves, but also for others. Again, it's part of the Master Plan. The purpose of life is found in becoming a better you while making our world a better place. This is the Higher Purpose – the one that directs us to work toward a greater good for ourselves as well as humanity. Though we find it hard to admit, all of life is *interdependent* – meaning everyone's choices **can and will** eventually affect the lives of others. Part of your Higher Purpose is to make good choices, to not only live and enjoy your life, but to leave a positive legacy for those with whom you share this world.

We are here to do what we are able to do – for the benefit of ourselves ***and*** *others.*

A meaningful life requires you to recognize that our world is one to be shared. We can never live happily and peacefully if we choose to live only for ourselves. True happiness and personal fulfillment comes from giving yourself to others while continuing to grow into a better you. If you define your purpose underneath this principle, and in accordance with your principle desires, you will find that true happiness is well within your reach. But even then, there is more to life than just high ideals. ***Purpose*** **without** ***goals*** **is useless** – like a plan with no action. This is where goal-setting helps bring your purpose to life.

Goal-Setting: Bringing Purpose to Life

Goal-setting is the actual process of defining your purpose, by exercising your *power of choice*. You see, life provides you with an incredible gift – opportunity. This opportunity leaves you with innumerable choices. Although this wealth of choices can seem overwhelming, in the grand scheme of things, these choices are all the power we have. **Goal-setting is the *conscious* exercise of choice**.

Goal-setting enables you to choose how you will take your passion and purpose to a higher level. Goal-setting leads you toward your desired result by helping you identify and plan to achieve what you want. With your achievement comes a sense of courage, confidence, and fulfillment we all strive to attain. Purpose and goal-setting work hand-in-hand to help us proactively better ourselves and our world. This is how we bring meaning to our lives and make life worth living.

When our life's journey has ended, and we've left this earth, all that is left is the lasting impressions of the choices we've made and the goals we've achieved. This is why, when defining your purpose, the most important question you can ask yourself is: "What impression do I want my life to leave?" This is the end result you want your life on earth to have. The answer you provide will reflect the goals you wish to achieve and the choices you should make, from this day on, throughout your life.

The Realization

Like you, I've made many choices in my life – some of them for the right reasons, some for the wrong reasons, and some for reasons I still don't understand. Each and every one of these choices have had some result, affecting not only me but countless others – both met and unmet. Some of these results I'm proud to admit, some I wish to forget, and some I may never know. But regardless, these results reflect the choices I've made. And when I'm gone, I'll be remembered for these results – for all that I've accomplished and all that I've said or done, no matter how good or how bad, how much or how little. These choices were, and still are, up to me. The same goes for you.

So to put it simply, your purpose is up to YOU. Define your reason for being and the answer to "Why am I here?" **by making a *conscious* choice**. Ask yourself: "What do I want the end result of my life to be?" Decide how you will live your life. Decide how you will better yourself, and better serve our world. Decide what you can and want to do in your life that is consistent with your higher purpose, your principle desires, your passions, and your abilities. These choices give you the power to find the happiness and fulfillment you've been looking for and expect out of life.

Now obviously, you can't take back the choices you've made in your past – but that makes no difference now. You can learn from the results of yesterday, make better choices today, and see better results tomorrow and each day of your life. That is the purpose of setting and reaching your goals – and *Discover Your Purpose* will show you how!

How to Use This Book

Discover Your Purpose is simple to use. Complete each exercise in the order it appears in the book. For your convenience, each exercise is complete with its own set of instructions – including the purpose of the exercise, general directions, and helpful hints. Certain exercises may use a "sample goal" to help you generate your own responses.

To help you succeed in the goal-setting process here, please consider the following advice:

- For the purpose of this book, we define a goal as something you wish to accomplish - NOT something you wish to acquire. DO NOT concern yourself with material things, as *true* happiness is NOT found in what you have, but by what you do.

- DO keep an open mind. No goal is too big or too small. You only need to *believe* in your goals in order to achieve them.

- DO use pencil when completing each exercise. Goal-setting is a process – and it is likely that some of your goals and/or priorities will change as you progress.

- DO read the Helpful Hints for each exercise BEFORE you begin to complete it. These hints will help you formulate your responses and better utilize the exercise.

- DO keep this book close at hand, *at all times*. It will soon become a reference point for your life – helping you gain a stronger sense of direction and a stronger sense of self.

- DO NOT give up! If you've decided on a goal that is truly important to you, believe in it and work for it! It's the only way to make it happen!

- DO NOT rush through this book! *Discover Your Purpose* is not meant to change your life overnight. Contemplation is the key to making this process work – and contemplation takes time. Look inside yourself. Think long and hard before you answer each question.

What is a Goal?

For the purpose of this book, a goal is defined as something you wish to accomplish – NOT something you wish to acquire. In this respect, a goal can be nearly anything you can possibly conceive. It is likely, however, that most your goals will fall into one of the following categories:

- **Personal Goals** – Goals that will strengthen your confidence by increasing your sense of self-worth, self-awareness, and personal achievement. These goals will help you become the best you can be. They may include: becoming more organized, becoming more disciplined, controlling your temper, practicing your faith, improving your communication skills, being more assertive without being aggressive, etc.

- **Health Goals** – Goals that will help you improve your overall health and well-being. These goals affect the present and future condition of your mind and body. They may include: losing weight, managing anxiety and depression, increasing your physical strength, increasing your flexibility, quitting smoking, etc.

- **Educational Goals** – Goals that will increase your knowledge and understanding of subjects you find pertinent, or just plain interesting. These goals will help you become competent in any subject you choose. They may include: studying politics, earning a degree, obtaining a professional license, improving your reading skills, etc.

- **Family Goals** – Goals that will help you create a stronger bond with your family. These goals will help you enrich your family life and will help you develop better one-on-one relationships with members of your family. They may include: understanding your parents, balancing work and family, becoming a better parent, solving marital issues, getting closer to your siblings, etc.

- **Relationship Goals** – Goals that will help you be a better friend and/or partner to someone you love or care about. These goals affect your daily interactions with others. They may include: learning to be more open, developing trust, avoiding arguments, improving your listening skills, etc.

- **Career Goals** – Goals that will help you find fulfilling work in your life that will suit your wants and needs, as well as allow you to utilize your greatest talents and strengths. They may include: starting a business, getting a promotion, increasing your sales, finding a new career, etc.

- **Humanitarian Goals** – Goals that will help you define how you will effect a positive change on the world. These goals can even be the focus of your career goals! They may include: counseling teens, saving the environment, feeding the hungry, caring for the sick, serving the community, etc.

Discover Yourself

Purpose

To help you learn more about who you are and want to become.

Directions

Read and answer each question by writing in your response. Then, read each of your responses aloud, and ask yourself, "Why?"

Helpful Hints

This is a time for deep, self-reflection. Answer each question as openly and honestly as possible, providing meaningful responses.

- Read each question carefully. Be sure that you understand each question *clearly* before you respond.
- Don't rush. Take your time when answering. Allow yourself *at least* ten minutes to answer each question.
- Be specific. The more specific you are with your responses, the more you will learn and understand about yourself.
- Be open. Record any and all responses that come to mind. Don't judge your responses – just record them. You'll have time to reflect on them later.
- For each question, record all of your responses FIRST. Then, ask yourself "Why?" This process will allow you to record as many answers as possible, for you to reflect on later.

Discover Yourself

What kinds of activities do you feel you are good at? Why?

What kinds of activities do you enjoy most? Why?

What subjects do you enjoy learning about? Why?

Discover Yourself

What strengths do you have that have helped you succeed in life? Why?

What weaknesses do you have that tend to interfere with your success? Why?

What people, ideas, beliefs, and/or material things do you value most in your life? Why?

Discover Yourself

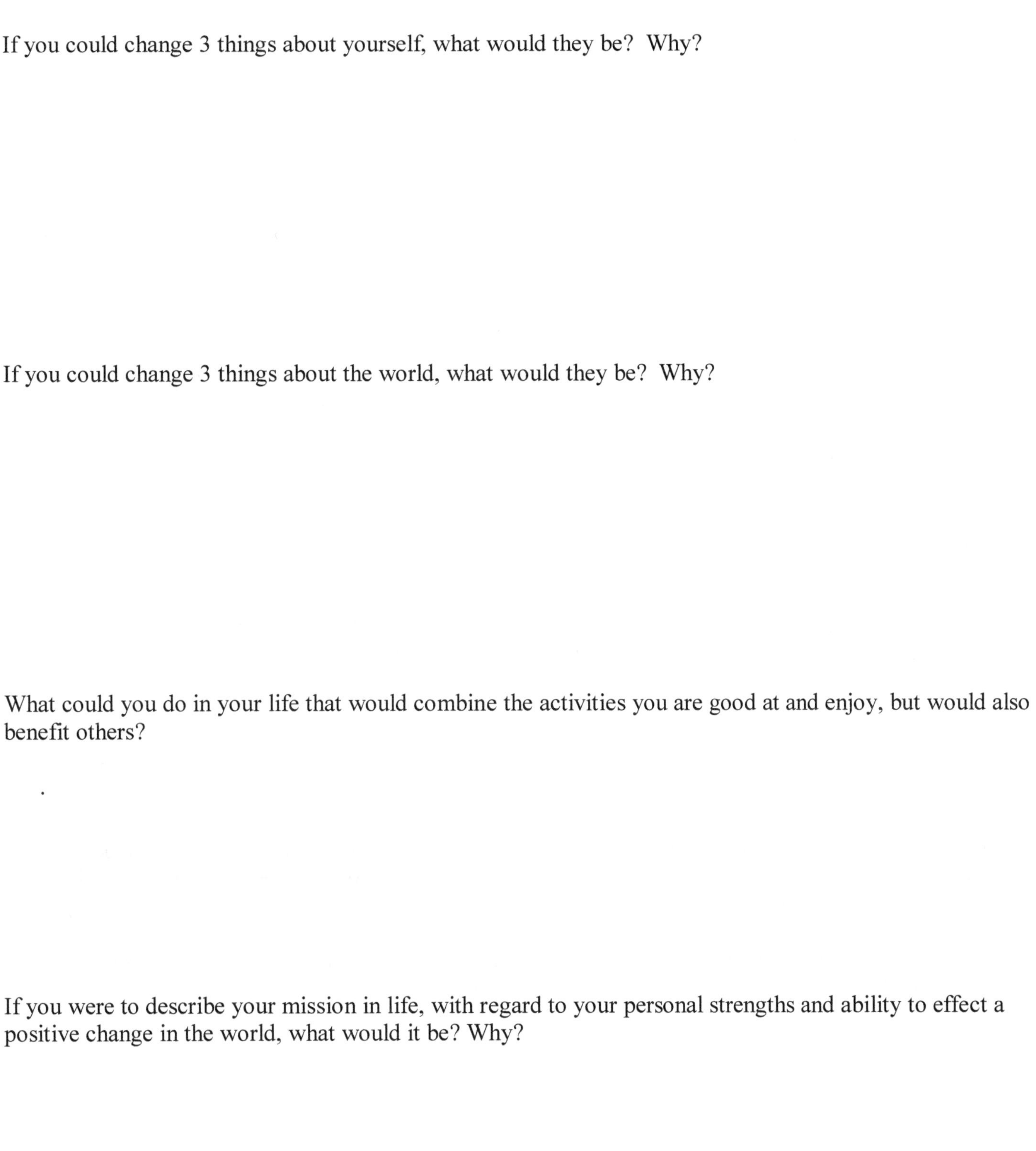

If you could change 3 things about yourself, what would they be? Why?

If you could change 3 things about the world, what would they be? Why?

What could you do in your life that would combine the activities you are good at and enjoy, but would also benefit others?

If you were to describe your mission in life, with regard to your personal strengths and ability to effect a positive change in the world, what would it be? Why?

Brainstorming

Purpose

To help you discover what you truly want out of life.

Directions

Write down EACH of your goals – no matter how big, how small, or how impractical it may seem. Then, when you have completed your list, circle the 10 goals you feel are most important to you *at this time*. Next, read these 10 goals aloud.

Helpful Hints

A goal is something you wish to accomplish – a desired result. It is a statement of what you want to *be*, to *do*, to *learn*, to *improve*, to *change*, or to *influence*.

- Spend *at least* 15 minutes on this exercise. Write down as many goals as you can - including personal, health, family, educational, relationship, career, and humanitarian goals.

- Write down *every* goal that comes to mind. Don't judge them! For now, no goal is too big, too small, or too impractical.

- Think of your *principle desires*: To know and understand yourself. To better yourself. To express yourself in your own unique way. To achieve by doing what you love and enjoy. To love, care for, and help each other. What goals come to mind?

- Refer back to your responses from the Discover Yourself exercise. These answers may give you some insight into the goals you wish to achieve, such as putting your strengths to better use, or turning a weakness into a strength!

- After exhausting your brainstorming session, go back and read through your list of goals. Is there anything that really jumps out at you? Is there anything that makes you excited to think about? These are likely to be the goals you will want to circle first.

- In the future, keep this book close at hand. You'll discover that new goals can (and will) come to mind at any time. Record them quickly so you don't lose sight of them.

Brainstorming

I want to…

Example: Start my own business.

Brainstorming

I want to…

Example: Start my own business.

Prioritizing

Purpose

To help you discover what is most important to you and why.

Directions

List each of your top 10 goals in order of importance. Then, next to each goal explain why this goal is ranked higher than the ones below it.

Helpful Hints

These 10 goals are at the top of your list for a reason. Take the time to identify these reasons and you will develop a greater commitment toward reaching them.

- Think carefully as you rank your goals. These goals now represent, above all else, who you want to become and what you want to accomplish. Ask yourself why.
- Be completely honest with yourself while ranking each goal. This is essential to successfully completing the goal-setting process.
- Goal #1 should represent something you want to achieve that will prove to you, when all is said and done, that your life was not in vain. It should represent your primary purpose in life.
- Goal #2 should represent a short-term, personal goal. This goal will become your motivation to complete the goal-setting process.
- Goals #3-10 should be ranked according to their importance in your life *at this time*. It is *essential* that you honestly identify *why* you have ranked these goals higher than the others. What makes them so important to you? Your answers will help you develop a stronger commitment toward reaching these goals. They may also reveal to you other goals related to your desired result.
- Be sure your goals are fairly specific. If not, you may want to reword them a little, to help you clarify the desired result you are looking for. If your goal is too general, you may find it difficult to create a plan to reach it.
- Remember: None of these goals are written in stone! As you progress through the book, you may decide to change the goals on your list, or even the priority of your goals. This is normal, and perfectly okay. This is the reason you should always use pencil when completing each exercise.
- Consider urgency. Which goals are most important *at this time*? You may have goals that you simply MUST achieve sooner than later – such as getting a job, passing a test, handling a marital issue, etc.

Prioritizing

Rank	Goal	Why?
Example:	To start my own cleaning business.	Because I'm tired of working for others. I want more freedom to dedicate my life to what I really enjoy.
#1		
#2		
#3		
#4		
#5		
#6		
#7		
#8		
#9		
#10		

Affirmations

Purpose

To strengthen your commitment toward reaching your goals.

Directions

Rewrite each of your top 10 goals beginning with the phrase "I WILL." Then, read each of these affirmations aloud.

Helpful Hints

At times, we all find it hard to motivate ourselves to act, even if it is in our best interest to do so. This exercise is a method of coaching your inner self – changing your focus from "This is what I *want* to do." to "This is what I *will* do."

- Start with your first affirmation. Read it aloud, over and over again, until you start to develop a feeling inside you that says, "I can do this! I can *really* do this!" It may take reading it aloud 5, 10, or even 20 times – but you *must* do it. This is how you develop confidence in your ability to reach your goal. Continue with each of your top 10 goals.

- Look at each of your affirmations. Believe that you can make them true. Start by repeating to yourself, "One step at a time. One step at a time."

- Stand in front of a mirror. Take a look at yourself, think of your affirmations and smile. Tell yourself, "I can do anything, if I do a little each day."

- Read your affirmations each and every day – several times a day! You are coaching yourself to succeed. You *must* remind yourself daily, and frequently, of what you will accomplish.

- Write your affirmations on note-cards and post them around your home and/or office. This will help you stay focused throughout the day, and remind you to read your affirmations aloud.

- Believe you have *already done* what you have set out to do. Even though your affirmations are written in the future tense, it helps to think of them as if you have already accomplished your goal. This is how you teach yourself to act in accordance with your goals – by embracing your goals as a reality, instead of just a dream. Then naturally, your choices will guide you to *maintain* and *magnify* your desired result.

Affirmations

Rank	Goal
Example:	I WILL start my own cleaning business.
#1	
#2	
#3	
#4	
#5	
#6	
#7	
#8	
#9	
#10	

Seeing is Believing

Purpose

To help you "SEE" your goals so clearly, you are driven to achieve them.

Directions

In the appropriate space, fill in your goal statement. Then, for each statement, visualize yourself reaching that goal. What do you see? Next, write a description of everything you can expect to "see" when you have reached your goal.

Helpful Hints

A goal is like a dream. With enough details, both can seem quite real. But with goals, you have the power to make them real, if you can see them clearly enough to believe they *can* be real.

- Visualization is one of the strongest techniques you can use in the goal-setting process. You should visualize not only the moment when your goal has been reached, but also the process leading up to it. Visualize the steps you will take to get you there.

- Relax as you visualize. This should be a pleasurable experience; not a chore. Enjoy the feelings you experience as you create a mental image of your success. If it helps, turn on some music to help you relax and think.

- Spend *at least* ten minutes (per goal) visualizing your success. How will you know when your goal has been reached? What measurements will you use to determine your success?

- Make your descriptions as detailed as possible. Who are you with? What are you doing? When and where does it happen? How does it occur? What are the results? The more real it seems to you, the more likely you are to achieve it.

- In your description, create a timetable for your success. Ask yourself, "When do I want to see this done by?" But PLEASE be realistic. Your goal *can* be reached, but it *will* take time. *Rome wasn't built in a day!*

- If possible, place visuals representing your goals around your home and/or office. Let them remind you where your goals will take you.

- Read over your descriptions daily. This will help you keep your goals "alive" in your mind, and will encourage your commitment to the goal-setting process.

Seeing is Believing

Example:

Goal: I will start my own business.

I will have a home-based cleaning business. I'll call my business "Don't Do It Yourself Cleaning Services". I'll have T-shirts made that I will use as my uniform. I'll have a fixed set of cleaning supplies that I know will work well for specific jobs. I will clean the homes of individuals and small offices. I'll have a set of business clients that I visit weekly to clean their bathrooms, hallways, and waiting areas. I will vacuum, dust and clean their windows and doors. I will have regular appointments to clean the homes of the elderly who are unable to do it themselves. I will pass out business cards to friends and family members. I'll have a contract I will use for each client. I'll have flyers posted in grocery stores and restaurants. I'll charge $12 per hour, to cover my labor and supplies. I'll have a plan to work quickly and efficiently. I'll have commercial insurance to cover any losses I may incur. I'll have a list of services that I provide, available to future clients to review. I'll be happy knowing I am helping others with their needs and getting paid what I'm worth.

Seeing is Believing

Goal #1 ____

Goal #2 ____

Seeing is Believing

Goal #3 ____

Goal #4 ____

Seeing is Believing

Goal #5 ____

Goal #6 ____

Seeing is Believing

Goal #7 ____

Goal #8 ____

Seeing is Believing

Goal #9 ____

Goal #10____

Overcoming Obstacles

Purpose

To help you identify any hurdles to your success; and to give you the confidence you CAN succeed.

Directions

For each goal, write down 5-10 obstacles which may stand in your way. Then, write down one or more ways you can overcome each obstacle.

Helpful Hints

Chances are your goals are not *entirely* unique. Others, just like you, have succeeded in reaching goals that are similar to yours. That means someone, somewhere, has faced many of the same obstacles, and still has overcome them. If you believe in yourself and plan as best as you can, you CAN overcome *your* obstacles as well.

- The first step to overcoming any obstacle is to identify it. Spend at least 10 minutes (per goal) contemplating what obstacles may stand in the way of your success. These obstacles will basically fall into two categories: Personal and External.

- Start by identifying your personal obstacles. These are obstacles that are within the realm of your control. Many of them, you'll find, are mental – including fear, procrastination, and negative attitudes. Some obstacles may include a lack of knowledge, poor time management, poor communication skills, etc. These too, can also be overcome, if you're willing to put forth the effort to do so. Determine how you can turn these weaknesses into strengths.

- Next, identify external obstacles. These may include: lack of available information, lack of money, lack of support from family and friends, competition, other people, etc. These obstacles may present a challenge, but often, it *is* possible to work around them. Ask others for advice – this is crucial.

- Recognize and *believe* that all of these obstacles CAN be overcome. To do so, you have to find the resources that will help you. This will take time *and* effort. But you can do it! Every step you take toward overcoming these obstacles is a reward in itself.

- There are plenty of resources available to you. You can find information pertaining to the subject or goal you are focused on in books, magazines, or on the Internet. Visit your local library or bookstore to see what you can find.

- Consider your family, friends, co-workers, professional contacts, and anyone you can find that has reached similar goals. Their knowledge and experience can give you insight on how you can best prepare to succeed.

- Pray. Sometimes we can find the answers we're seeking when we quiet ourselves, ask for guidance, and just listen. You'd be surprised at the answers that may come, when you open your heart and mind.

Overcoming Obstacles

Example: I will start my own business.

Obstacles	How Will I Overcome?
I don't know what it takes to start a cleaning business.	I'll contact my local chapter of SCORE for free advice on starting a business.
I don't have money for advertising.	I'll ask some friends to print off flyers that I can put up in grocery stores and restaurants.
I'm nervous about taking on the responsibility.	I'll work on getting just one, regular client first (preferably a friend) to help me get comfortable with the work involved.
I'm not very organized.	I'll buy a planner. I'll ask a friend to help me plan how to get myself more organized.
I don't know how to talk to people.	I'll talk to my friends and ask them to get me referrals, so I don't have to do the initial contact. I'll write and memorize a short script, describing the services I will offer.

Overcoming Obstacles

Goal #1 ____

Obstacles	How Will I Overcome?

Overcoming Obstacles

Goal #2 ____

Obstacles	How Will I Overcome?

Overcoming Obstacles

Goal #3 ____

Obstacles	How Will I Overcome?

Overcoming Obstacles

Goal #4 ____

Obstacles	How Will I Overcome?

Overcoming Obstacles

Goal #5 ____

Obstacles	How Will I Overcome?

Overcoming Obstacles

Goal #6 ____

Obstacles	How Will I Overcome?

Overcoming Obstacles

Goal #7 ______________________________

Obstacles	How Will I Overcome?

Overcoming Obstacles

Goal #8 ____

Obstacles	How Will I Overcome?

Overcoming Obstacles

Goal #9 ____________________

Obstacles	How Will I Overcome?

Overcoming Obstacles

Goal #10 ____

Obstacles	How Will I Overcome?

Creating Objectives

Purpose

To help you identify the actions you must take to reach your goals.

Directions

For each goal, write down 5-10 objectives you plan to complete that will help you reach your goal. Then, assign a deadline for each objective. Lastly, write down why and how each objective will help you reach your goal.

Helpful Hints

Everything you do should have a reason – a purpose of its own. The purpose of any action should be to lead you closer to achieving your desired result; otherwise, you'll be wasting your energy.

- You may need more than the allotted space to record your objectives. Brainstorm as many pertinent objectives as possible, before completing the "Why?" column. Feel free to use additional paper. Take the time to make a solid, *detailed* plan to achieve your desired result.

- Have fun with this exercise. The completion of every objective is an achievement of its own. Just imagine how much you'll have accomplished, even as you work toward the completion of your goals.

- Be specific. What actions must you take in order to reach your goal? How will you do it? How often? Once? Daily? Weekly? Why is it important?

- In your description of each objective, include a deadline. How long will you give yourself to complete your objective? Be reasonable. Consider buying a planner to help you schedule your deadlines.

- Here's a suggestion – If your objective will take you longer than *two weeks* to complete, try to break it down into smaller parts, *or* turn that objective into a goal of its own.

- Refer back to the exercise Overcoming Obstacles. Use your responses to help you create objectives that will ensure your success. Make it your objective to overcome the obstacles you have listed.

- The most important objective for any goal is *research*. You can find advice on how to do practically anything through books, magazines, the Internet, family, friends, co-workers, professional contacts, and many other sources. You can also seek advice from people you don't currently know. Write a letter, send an email, or visit an office of someone you feel can give you the advice and knowledge you think you need. Many people who have succeeded in reaching their own goals, will be glad to help you plan to reach yours. But be prepared for rejection. Don't let "no" keep you from asking someone else. Your persistence will help you succeed.

- Read your objectives *each and every* day! Remember: You can do *anything*, one step at a time, and a little each day. When you read your objectives, cross off the ones you've completed, and congratulate yourself on your accomplishment. To start, focus on one goal at a time.

Creating Objectives

Example: I will start my own business.

Objective	Why?
Visit my local chapter of SCORE.	To get free, one-on-one, business startup advice.
Research information on starting a cleaning business at the local library and online.	I need some idea of the steps I should take to be successful in this type of business.
Write a business plan	It will help me better organize my business and define how I want my business to grow.
Write a list of services I plan to offer.	So I can know what I am willing and able to do to serve my customers and answer any questions they may have.
Register my business.	This will be required by law and may even give me some tax benefits.
Write a contract for customers.	This will explain the terms of my service so I can avoid any misunderstandings or arguments.
Ask my friends if they would like to become clients, or if they could give me a referral.	This will help me to gradually get accustomed to the type of work I want to do, and will raise my confidence.

Creating Objectives

Goal #1 ____

Objective	Why?

Creating Objectives

Goal #2 ____

Objective	Why?

Creating Objectives

Goal #3 ____________________

Objective	Why?

Creating Objectives

Goal #4 ____

Objective	Why?

Creating Objectives

Goal #5 ____

Objective	Why?

Creating Objectives

Goal #6 ____

Objective	Why?

Creating Objectives

Goal #7 ____

Objective	Why?

Creating Objectives

Goal #8 ____

Objective	Why?

Creating Objectives

Goal #9 ____

Objective	Why?

Creating Objectives

Goal #10____

Objective	Why?

Planning Your Rewards

Purpose

To help you find the motivation to complete your objectives and reach your goals.

Directions

Write down various ways you can reward yourself when you complete an objective. Then, for each objective you complete, select one item from your list as a celebration of your accomplishment.

Helpful Hints

Every achievement deserves a reward of some kind. Granted, success is a great reward for your hard work, but you should also *enjoy yourself* along the way. Plan rewards for completing your objectives, so you have something to look forward to as you work toward your goals.

- Think about your favorite pastimes. Now, consider these "reward only" pastimes. That means you can only enjoy them if you complete at least one of your objectives.
- Relax and unwind. Give yourself time to take a much needed nap, a bubble bath, or read a chapter or two from your favorite book.
- Cater to yourself. Plan a professional massage, a manicure/pedicure, a visit to the salon for a new haircut, etc.
- Get out of the house. You can take a walk, go to a concert, see a movie, visit the zoo, relax in the park, etc.
- Give yourself a gift. Buy yourself a new outfit, a CD, jewelry, or something else you would appreciate.
- Treat Yourself. Indulge in your favorite meal or dessert. Perhaps your favorite latte or specialty drink would be a pleasant reward.

Planning Your Rewards

My Personal Rewards	

Accomplishments

Purpose

To help you recognize and record your personal success.

Directions

For each goal you accomplish, re-write your goal statement under Accomplishments, beginning with the phrase "I have…"

Helpful Hints

Congratulations! You have successfully completed the goal-setting process. It's time for you to recognize your success and revel in the excitement of knowing you have accomplished something worthwhile.

- Realize this accomplishment is just the beginning! There is so much more you can do if you put your mind to it and plan as best as you can. Go back and begin working on your other goals. See for yourself how much more you can achieve!
- Tell others about your success! Knowing others can respect your accomplishments will boost your confidence and self-esteem.
- Read your list of accomplishments daily. This exercise is meant to remind you of the power you have to reach your goals and to help build your self-esteem.

Accomplishments

Example: I HAVE started my own cleaning business!

Conclusion

I hope you have found *Discover Your Purpose* to be a practical resource in helping you set and reach your personal goals. Let me take this time to remind you of what you have accomplished by completing this book…

- You have learned a lot about yourself. You've learned to analyze what makes you who you are. You've become more conscious of your strengths, weaknesses, values, desires, and concerns. You've acknowledged what you truly want out of life, and what matters to you.

- You have discovered your purpose – to use who you are to better yourself, and to better serve your world. You've learned that it is essential to recognize that the life you choose to lead affects not only you, but others as well. You've learned that living life with a higher purpose benefits us all.

- You've learned how to use the goal-setting process to plan your personal success. You have designed a plan to reach 10 of your most important goals, and have developed greater confidence in your ability to achieve them.

You can now take the knowledge you've obtained and apply it to any part of your life – making it richer, more rewarding, and more fulfilling. Knowledge is true power - and at the very least, by completing this book you should feel empowered to make a positive change in your life and find the happiness you deserve.

Congratulations, on all that you *have* accomplished and all that you *will* accomplish. Good luck with the rest of your journey…

From the Author

I began writing *Discover Your Purpose* in 2004. Its aim was to simplify the process of goal-setting, and make it more interactive – not just a subject you read about, get inspired by, and soon forget. I wanted to create a step-by-step process, which would allow for the immediate application of each goal-setting skill.

You set a goal and you reach it, right? It's not always as easy as it sounds. There are several steps in between. If you skip a step, you substantially reduce your chances of reaching that goal. Therefore, you must learn the process, and put it to work. *Reading* about the process is not the same as *doing* it. *Doing* is the focus of *Discover Your Purpose* – and that is why it works. I know firsthand.

There was a time in my life when I truly believed I had hit rock bottom. My life was at its worse, and it seemed like nothing was getting better. I cried and cried. I beat myself up. I tried to numb the pain, but I was still at a loss. Finally, I asked my Father in Heaven – what I now believe may have been just the right question – "Where did *I* go wrong?"

That's when it came to me –my life was in its present condition because of *my* choice. Whether it was the wrong choice, or lack of making a choice at all – I had, for all intents and purposes "dug my own grave" and allowed myself to end up where I did. Of course, there had been circumstances that were beyond my control and that had knocked me down to my knees; but *I had the choice* to pick myself up – and I had chosen not to.

So I realized (I believe by God's divine intervention) that it was time for a change. I had to make a positive change in my life, by making better, more positive, and more conscious choices. That's when I began my study of goal-setting. I literally read dozens of books and hundreds of articles. Some of them were helpful, many of them inspiring, but none of them gave me exactly what I was looking for – a simple, practical guide to goal-setting, that could explain, succinctly and directly, how to set and reach my goals. After failing to find a single resource that could meet my expectations, I was led to do the next best thing – create one of my own.

Discover Your Purpose uses all the techniques you'll find in many self-help books, but without the fluff and long-winded discussions. It gets straight to the point and provides a simple answer to a simple question – "How do I set and reach my goals?"

I hope this book is as much of a blessing to you as it was for me. I still keep mine beside me, at all times, to keep me focused on achieving *my* desired result.

Acknowledgements

This book is very special to me. *Discover Your Purpose* is not only my first published book, it is also my personal blessing.

When my life had reached its lowest point, I was ready to give up. I was lost and hurting. I felt I was no more than a perfect failure. "Where did I go wrong?" After 23 years, my life had no real meaning and I had no purpose. I didn't even have a dream. "Where can I possibly go from here?"

Many days I cried - at first, only on the inside. Then one day, I broke down and found myself crying out for help. "God, help me! Tell me why I'm here? What am I supposed to do? All I want is to be happy, but I just don't know how!"

After sitting alone, quietly, for what seemed like an eternity, I felt the urge to pick up a pen and notebook. I started to write. I don't know where the thoughts came from, but I began to write furiously, my pen burning across the page. By the end of what must have been about an hour-long writing session, I had laid the groundwork for what became the premise of this book. It was my personal guide to finding my path.

I call *Discover Your Purpose* my spiritual gift. It helped me to think more consciously and proactively. It helped me identify how special God had made me. It helped me realize He had indeed created me with a purpose; and it was to serve Him. All I needed to do was use the gifts He had already given me to grow - through my conscious desire to better myself and through my service to others.

All these years, I had failed to recognize that I can take what I love to do most – writing – and use it to serve both myself *and* others. And as I began to do this, I felt like a window to my life had been opened. Like the light was finally coming in. I had found my purpose, and it had been with me all along. I only had to put it to use.

I am thankful to God for *Discover Your Purpose*. It was an inspiration and an answer to my prayers. It helped me to refocus my life and see clearly what I was meant to do. In light of this, I don't much care to think of myself as the *author* of this book. Perhaps it would be more right for me to say that even at my very best, I'm only just the messenger.

-Angel

www.ingramcontent.com/pod-product-compliance
Lightning Source LLC
LaVergne TN
LVHW061256100826
845148LV00008B/1145